I0485485

Marketing Skills For Product Managers

How Product Managers Can Use Marketing To Make Their Product A Success

"Practical, proven examples of how to use your marketing skills to make your product a success!"

Dr. Jim Anderson

Published by:
Blue Elephant Consulting
Tampa, Florida

Printed in the United States of America

Library of Congress Control Number: 2015915614

ISBN-13: 978-1517468736

ISBN-10: 1517468736

Warning – Disclaimer

Recent Books By The Author

Product Management

- Product Management Secrets: Techniques For Product Managers To Boost Product Sales And Increase Customer Satisfaction

- Customer Lessons For Product Managers: Techniques For Product Managers To Better Understand What Their Customers Really Want

Public Speaking

- How To Become A Better Speaker By Changing How You Speak: Change techniques that will transform a speech into a memorable event

- How To Give A Great Presentation: Presentation techniques that will transform a speech into a memorable event

CIO Skills

- What CIOs Need To Know About Working With Partners: Techniques For CIOs To Use In Order To Be Able To Successfully Work With Partners

- How CIOs Can Make Innovation Happen: Tips And Techniques For CIOs To Use In Order To Make Innovation Happen In Their IT Department

IT Manager Skills

- How IT Managers Can Make Innovation Happen: Tips And Techniques For IT Managers To Use In Order To Make Innovation Happen In Their Teams

- Secrets Of Effective Leadership For IT Managers: Tips And Techniques That IT Managers Can Use In Order To Develop Leadership Skills

Negotiating

- Learn How To Package Trades In Your Next Negotiation

- Learn How To Signal In Your Next Negotiation: How To Develop The Skill Of Effective Signaling In A Negotiation In Order To Get The Best Possible Outcome

Miscellaneous

- The Internet-Enabled Successful School District Superintendent: How To Use The Internet To Boost Parental Involvement In Your Schools

- Power Distribution Unit (PDU) Secrets: What Everyone Who Works In A Data Center Needs To Know!

Note: See a complete list of books by Dr. Jim Anderson at the back of this book.

Acknowledgements

Any book like this one is the result of years of real-world work experience. In my over 25 years of working for 7 different firms, I have met countless fantastic people and I've been mentored by some truly exceptional ones. Although I've probably forgotten some of the people who made me the person that I am today, here is my attempt to finally give them the recognition that they so truly deserve:

- Thomas P. Anderson
- Art Puett
- Bobbi Marshall
- Bob Boggs

Dr. Jim Anderson

This book is dedicated to my wife Lori. None of this would have been possible without her love and support.

Thanks for the best 24 years of my life (so far)...!

Speaking.   Negotiating.   Managing.   Marketing.

Table Of Contents

To Sell A Product, You Have To Market It

At the heart of what it means to be a product manager lies the ability to market your product. No matter if you are trying to get people inside of your company to provide you with the resources or funding that your product needs in order to get out the door or if its customers that you are after, you've got to be able to paint a picture of your product that makes people want it.

Product managers are not perfect and when it comes to marketing our product, we do make mistakes. However, the key is to learn from both our mistakes and the mistakes that other product managers have made in order to ensure that we won't be repeating them. Not making mistakes is even more important now that the Web 2.0 has arrived. Everything that we do in terms of marketing our product can now be instantly seen by the rest of the world.

When we meet with customers, we present out product in the best light possible. More often than not we use either PowerPoint or Keynote slides to do this. However, have any of us ever gotten any training on how to make really good slides? If not, then we should seek it out in order to help our products. How our products look on those slides is the key to getting a customer to want the product. This means that we need a basic understanding of the color wheel and how different colors either work together – or don't!

When economic times get tough, inside of your company they are going to be looking for people who can help the company out. This is the time for a product manager to step up and show the company how his or her product can positively impact the company's bottom line. One way to go about making this happen is to create a website for your product that actually works and is not just another online advertising brochure.

For more information on what it takes to be a great product manager, check out my blog, The Accidental Product Manager, at:

www.TheAccidentalPM.com

Good luck!

-    Dr. Jim Anderson

About The Author

I must confess that I never set out to be a product manager. When I went to school, I studied Computer Science and thought that I'd get a nice job programming and that would be that. Well, at least part of that plan worked out!

My first job was working for Boeing on their F/A-18 fighter jet program. I spent my days programming fighter jet software in assembly language and I loved it. The U.S. government decided to save some money and went looking for other countries to sell this plane to. This put me into an unfamiliar role: I started to meet with foreign military officials in order to explain what my product did.

Time moved on and so did I. I found myself working for Siemens, the big German telecommunications company. They were making phone switches and selling them to the seven U.S. phone companies. The problem was that the switches were too complicated. Customers couldn't tell the difference between one complicated phone switch from another complicated phone switch.

The Siemens sales folks were in a bind. They didn't know enough about how the switches worked to tell their customers why they should buy them. Siemens reached out into their engineering unit looking for anyone who could help the sales teams out. I put my hand up and overnight I became a product manager.

Since then I've spent over 20 years working as a product manager for both big companies and startups. This has given me an opportunity to do everything that a product manager does many, many times. I know what works as well as what doesn't work.

I now live in Tampa Florida where I spend my time managing my consulting business, Blue Elephant Consulting, teaching college courses at the University of South Florida, and traveling to work with companies like yours to share the knowledge that I have about how product managers can make their product be a success.

I'm always available to answer questions and I can be reached at:

Dr. Jim Anderson
Blue Elephant Consulting
Email: jim@BlueElephantConsulting.com
Facebook: http://goo.gl/1TVoK
Web: **www.BlueElephantConsulting.com**

"Unforgettable communication skills that will set your ideas free..."

Create Products Your Customers Want At A Price That They Are Willing To Pay!

Dr. Jim Anderson is available to provide training and coaching on the two topics that are the most important to product managers everywhere: how do I create the products that my customers want and what should I price them at?

Dr. Anderson believes that in order to both learn and remember what he says, product managers need to laugh. Each one of his speeches is full of fun and humor so that what he says "sticks" with everyone.

Dr. Anderson's Product Management Training Includes:

1. How can you segment your market?
2. What problems are your customers having right now?
3. Which of your customer's problems does your product solve?
4. How much of this problem does your product solve?
5. How much will it cost your customer if they don't fix this problem?

Dr. Jim Anderson presents over 100 speeches per year. To invite Dr. Anderson to speak at your event, contact him at:

Phone: 813-418-6970 or
Email: jim@BlueElephantConsulting.com

Blue
Elephant
Consulting
Speaking. Negotiating. Managing. Marketing.

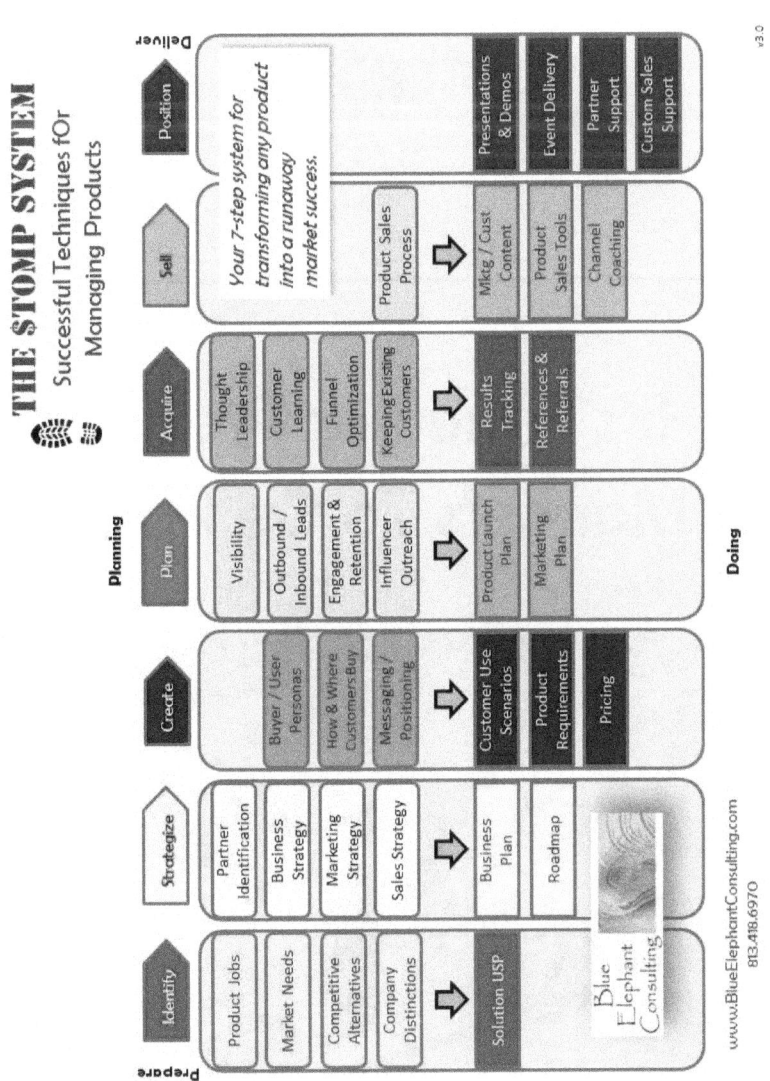

THE $TOMP SYSTEM
Successful Techniques fOr Managing Products

Your 7-step system for transforming any product into a runaway market success.

Identify	Strategize	Create	Plan	Acquire	Sell	Position
Product Jobs	Partner Identification	Buyer / User Personas	Visibility	Thought Leadership	Product Sales Process	Presentations & Demos
Market Needs	Business Strategy	How & Where Customers Buy	Outbound / Inbound Leads	Customer Learning		Event Delivery
Competitive Alternatives	Marketing Strategy	Messaging / Positioning	Engagement & Retention	Funnel Optimization		Partner Support
Company Distinctions	Sales Strategy		Influencer Outreach	Keeping Existing Customers		Custom Sales Support
Solution USP	Business Plan	Customer Use Scenarios	Product Launch Plan	Results Tracking	Mktg / Cust Content	
	Roadmap	Product Requirements	Marketing Plan	References & Referrals	Product Sales Tools	
		Pricing			Channel Coaching	

Prepare — Planning — Doing — Deliver

www.BlueElephantConsulting.com
813.418.6970

v3.0

The **$TOMP** product management system has been created by **Blue Elephant Consulting** to help product managers know what to do and when to do it in order for a product to be successful.

Chapter 1

It's Time For Product Mangers To Go Postal

Chapter 1: It's Time For Product Mangers To Go Postal

How cool is it that we get to live in this all-digital, all-electronic 21st Century? Given all of the tools that a product manager has available to him/her, we should be having no problems getting information on our products out to existing / prospective customers, right? Wrong! Our customers are overloaded and so we've got our work cut out for us...

Perhaps this is a good time for us to talk about DM. You know, Direct Mail.

"What?" you scoff. "You mean all that junk that I throw away every day when I come home and go through my mail?" Yes – that stuff. However, before you go getting on your high horse and telling me that you would never consider besmirching the fine name of your product / brand / company by stooping to using Direct Mail, maybe you should stop and think for just a moment.

Google's AdSense ads that you see are just another form of direct mail and they sure seem to be doing well for the company.

You really don't care about the people who throw your direct mail pieces away. What you care about is the people who open them and read them. These may be potential buyers who turn into actual customers.

In a world that is overrun with emails, IMs, tweets, etc., there is something strangely comforting in holding in your hand a real piece of advertising material – it somehow makes what's being pitched all that more real.

If I've been able to convince you that direct mail might be a new way to reach out to potential customers that you have not been able to get to consider your product any other way, then the next question out of your mouth should be "how?"

The first rule of fight club is... Oh wait, that's a different movie. The first rule of direct marketing is that you must not practice deception. All too often it's easy to get caught up in a numbers game where you'll do almost anything to get more people to open up your direct mail piece. You've seen direct mail that didn't live up to this standard: they come with the words "You are a lottery winner!" or "Important Information About Your Account" on the outside of an envelope. Don't do this.

So what's a product manager to do? Here are 5 tips to help you set up and run a successful direct marketing campaign for your product:

1. **Know Your Mail:** Postal mail is good for some things and not good for other things. You need to make sure that the people who are getting your direct mail piece feel that they are getting something that they can use – not just another ad. Remember that we now live in green times and so you don't want to get in trouble for wasting paper.

2. **Make It Personal**: Since we are living in the 21st Century we do have access to databases and opt-in campaigns that can provide us with a lot of information about the people that we are sending our direct mail to. Make sure that you segment your audience data and send tailored pieces to them.

3. **Keep It Clean**: The outside of the envelope that you send your direct mail in is often treated like a side of the road billboard: extra text, a big logo, or all sorts of artwork. Don't do this! Instead, keep it simple and just

include the standards: an address, a return address, and a small logo.

4. **Make Quick Decisions Easy To Make**: Assuming that you've been able to get your audience to open up your direct mail piece, they're not going to be willing to spend a lot of time looking through it. Use clear graphics and tight copy to get your message across quickly. This will help your reader to prioritize the importance of what you've sent them.

5. **Pick Your Words Carefully**: Once again, you've entered a minefield here. Certain words have been overused in direct mail (think "free", think "new"). Pick your words very carefully so that they leave a lasting impression in your customer's minds while not ticking them off.

Chapter 2

Product Manager Marketing Mistakes

Chapter 2: Product Manager Marketing Mistakes

Where did you learn your marketing skills? At school? On the job? Never learned it? I've got some bad news for you: a lot of what you know may no longer be correct. A lot of what serves as conventional wisdom in the world of marketing is based on the way that things used to be. However, there have been a number of breakthroughs in the understanding of consumer behavior and this changes everything...

Lots of companies suspect that a lot of the money that they spend on marketing is being wasted. Why is this? When you spend dollars based on bad marketing concepts, you can pretty much kiss that money goodbye.

Let's discuss where product marketing has gone wrong and what we can do to fix things:

Mistake: Product managers should find and target market segments for their brands.

This is classic product management thinking – you need to identify and target the specific market segments that might be interested in buying your product. But wait, this kind of thinking can cause you to target too small of a set of potential customers.

It turns out that many customers, both consumers and business customers, are what researchers refer to as "repertoire customers" – they buy several brands regularly. Case in point: who made the cell phone that you have right now? Do you only buy cell phones that come from that manufacturer? I know that I started with Nokia, went to Motorola, and now I carry a LG. I'll go back to the others if price / features appeal to me when I'm shopping for my next cell phone.

One way for product managers to take advantage of repertoire buyers is to offer lots of brands and variants within the same product categories. This will allow you to capture more of the buyers as they purchase a repertoire of products.

Mistake: Loyal customers are your best customers.

You would think so, but it turns out that this is not true when you are dealing with repertoire customers. Studies have been done that show that it turns out that really only about 10% of customers can be considered to be loyal customers. Additionally, it turns out that they actually buy your product less frequently than non-loyal customers do. Clearly, loyal customers may not be where you want to be spending your marketing dollars.

Mistake: There are three ways to boost the growth of your brand – get more customers, make customers more loyal, and get customers to buy more often.

Oops, it turns out that there is really only one way to grow the sales of your brand – get more customers. This means that you need to either get more people in your existing markets to buy your product or you need to enter into new markets.

As product managers we often become worried when we see existing customers buying from our competition. We will quickly start dreaming up ways to stop our other customers from leaving us. Additionally, we start looking for ways to get our existing customers to purchase more often from us in order to make up for the customers that we've lost. Can anyone say slash prices?

Turns out that this is all a waste of time. When you are dealing with repertoire customers it's actually quite natural for them to buy from your competition over time. Studies show that actions on your part to stop them from leaving rarely work and more often than not end up damaging you.

The way to deal with this situation is to work on gaining market share for your product by acquiring new customers. Don't waste your time trying to win customer loyalty or get them to buy more often.

Chapter 3

How Product Managers Can Maximize Marketing

Chapter 3: How Product Managers Can Maximize Marketing

In order to have a successful product, you need to convince people to buy your product in the first place. We like to call this marketing. The problem is that lots of money can be spent on marketing with no real apparent return on the investment. Let's take a look at what product managers should NOT be doing...

Mistake: Assuming that in order for your product to be successful, it will need to be differentiated from its competition.

Different? Why bother? Sure if you are selling iPhones this is probably the case, but then how many of us are doing that? Nope, more often than not there is somebody in your product category that has got it all figured out. If there is no way that they can serve the whole market, then go ahead and copy them – you'll pick up the customers that they miss.

Mistake: Using promotions.

Don't let sales talk you into this one. Promotions have been shown to attract folks who won't remain long term customers and you end up just giving your steady customers a discount on something that they would have bought anyway.

Mistake: You must go out and capture new customers.

Yeah – back in the 1980's. Nowadays the shoe is on the other foot, what you really want to have happen is to have your customers show up and capture you. This means that the role of the product manager is to make sure that your customers can find your product and that when they do, you respond to them in a way that causes them to buy.

Chapter 4

How To Use Web 2.0 To Be A Better Product Manager

Chapter 4: How To Use Web 2.0 To Be A Better Product Manager

Right off the bat, I need to apologize for using "Web 2.0" in the title. It was a cheap trick to get you to read at least this far, but it sure seems to have worked. With all of that out of the way, hype aside, it sure does look like the Internet is changing how a product manager markets his / her product. Does anyone have any rules about how this needs to be done?

Since the phrase "Web 2.0" has been so abused by now, we should probably take a moment and make sure that we're all on the same page. I'm going to define Web 2.0 as simply being a new set of web-based tools that allow product mangers to build social and business connections (online), share information both internally and externally, and collaborate with colleagues and customers (online). Now how do you use these shiny new tools?

Web 2.0 tools offer product mangers a great way to convince customers to buy your product. The trick is that unlike traditional marketing you don't talk TO your potential customers, instead you try to get them INVOLVED in a discussion with you. Sounds rather dangerous doesn't it?

If you want to be able to talk to your (potential) customers, then you are going to need a Web 2.0 Wiki or Blog. Next, you are going to have to start writing – what can you tell people about your product that they may not already know?

Getting some interesting conversations going with your customer will start things off. Where things really start to get interesting is when your customers start to talk to each other. This is where product managers can find out what new features customers are really looking for and what they don't like about the current product.

In the old days, before Web 2.0 tools came along, product managers had to use focus groups and surveys to get feedback from our customers. Now all we have to do is post a question on the Web and we can get instant feedback. Ain't progress grand?

Chapter 5

How Product Managers Can Get Better At Creating PowerPoint Slides

Chapter 5: How Product Managers Can Get Better At Creating PowerPoint Slides

Yeah, yeah I know that everyone says that they hate Powerpoint – "death by Powerpoint" and all of that. However, the reality of modern Product Manger life is that we end up using Powerpoint to communicate a lot of information about our products and the current status of our projects. Thank goodness you took all of those Powerpoint classes back in college...

What? You've never had a Powerpoint class in your life? Hmm, can I at least assume that you know about the color wheel? Dang – struck out there also? Looks like we're going to have to have a talk here.

There are some people out there that are really gifted artists. One that comes to mind is Garr Reynolds over at Presentation Zen. However, then there is the rest of us. Powerpoint has a bunch of flashy features that lots of people like to use; however, the key is to remember that it's really a communication tool. This means that you'd like to get good enough at using it that you can get your point across in a clear way that will stick with your audience.

So how does a product manager go about doing this? It's actually pretty simple – it will just take an investment in time. I would suggest that you find a Powerpoint presentation that you've seen that really worked for you – it communicated what it was trying to say in a concise, clear way. Then you need to sit down with a blank Powerpoint presentation and try to recreate it from scratch.

This is actually a lot harder than it might seem at first, getting all of the details of a presentation that someone else created (fonts, colors, line thicknesses, what goes on top of what else, etc.) can be a challenge. However, as you go through this copy / creation process you'll discover how a really good presentation comes together.

Chapter 6

You Don't Do a Good Product Managers & The Secret Of The Color Wheel

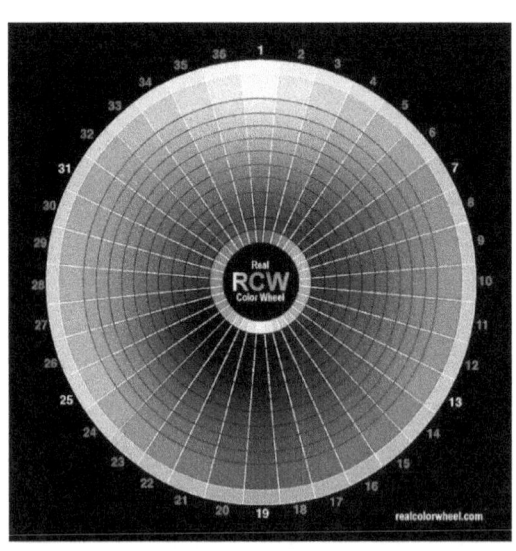

Chapter 6: Product Managers & The Secret Of The Color Wheel

So I'm just a little bit off the beaten path with this discussion, but I've recently had to sit through so many bad presentations that I'm feeling an overwhelming need to try to make the world a better place for Powerpoint slides to live in.

We all live and die by Powerpoint. I can't begin to tell you how many bosses that I've had that insisted that I provide them with status updates in Powerpoint form. What part of my hero Edward Tuff's write up after the Space Shuttle Challenger disaster ("Powerpoint Does Rocket Science") did they not read?

Well no matter, we have to do what we have to do. However, at the very least we should be able to do it to the best of our ability. One of the greatest errors that I've been seeing as of late is the criminal use of colors that in no way should ever be used together. Look, I realize that for most of us (guys) getting dressed in the morning can be a challenge (what goes with what), but we should have the same level of concern when it comes to creating slides.

So how should a product manager pick colors for his/her Powerpoint slides? Simple – use a color wheel. Using a color wheel and just a bit of color theory, a product manager can start to produce professional looking slides. It turns out that using analogous colors (colors that are next to each other on the color wheel) or complementary colors (colors are across from each other on the color wheel) are easy ways to get your colors right.

Thanks to the Internet, there are now free sites that if you need to start with one color (company color, product color) they will allow you to find out what colors work with that color. If this all seems to be too much for you, then you can visit the "Colors On

The Web" site and press the button in order to get a random color scheme that has matching colors created for you.

Chapter 7

Product Mangers Need A Dictionary In Order To Make Money

Chapter 7: Product Mangers Need A Dictionary In Order To Make Money

One of my favorite lines from Steve Martin's stand-up act goes like this "What's up with those French? It seems like they have a **different word** for everything..."

Perhaps many of us Product Managers have some French blood in us because it sure seems like we often get accused of willy-nilly making up new acronyms on the fly. In all honesty, yes we do do this sometimes. However, there is a more subtle word problem that has been creeping around the edges of the product management world for a long time that nobody's been brave enough to bring up: **we have no idea what we are saying**.

Ranjay Gulati, James Oldroyd, and Phanish Puranam are three researchers who have been studying this problem and they've made some interesting discoveries. Specifically, they've discovered that we all seem to THINK that we are talking about the same thing when in many cases we really aren't.

As product mangers we have to interact with many different departments. In order to meet the needs of all of these internal customers, product managers are always creating new and different ways to present the product information that we have. However, since nobody talks to anyone else in the company, we've been creating **a million different ways** to present (and talk about) the same product data.

What's been missing from the product manger's bag of communication tricks is some sort of **dictionary**. We need to standardize how we talk about our product's data and how we describe the results of the processing that we do on that data.

Over at Best Buy, Robert Willett who is their CIO said that when he first showed up they had **400 to 500 different ways to**

measure things. What this meant is that measurements done for one customer could not be interpreted by another customer so they had to do the processing all over again.

Robert spent over 10 months and drove things to a point where they had single definitions for everything. It was only after this type of process dictionary had been created that Best Buy started to **get some value** for all of its efforts. Getting value is how product managers can make more money and that will benefit us all.

Chapter 8

Web 2.0 Rules: Sell, Sell, Sell (Or Not)!

Chapter 8: Web 2.0 Rules: Sell, Sell, Sell (Or Not)!

Come on, 'fess up - you have just a little bit of a **salesperson** living inside of you. On those occasions that you get in front of a customer, you can hardly help yourself from launching into a "sales mode" and trying to convince the customer that they need your product. Now that the Web 2.0 has arrived, you can start to do this 24×7 right? Wrong.

Ranjay Gulati, James Oldroyd, and Phanish Puranam are three researchers who have been studying this problem and they've made some interesting discoveries. It turns out that your customers who are using Web 2.0 tools don't WANT you to hit them over the head with the **sales club**. Go figure.

These here online communities are a delicate thing. There is nothing MAKING your customers participate. Instead, you need to make them **WANT to participate**. One of the quickest ways to drive them away once they've joined is to go ahead and open up on them with your sales cannon.

What your customers are expecting you to do are two things: **listen and communicate**. This is something that a leading consumer-electronics company found out. They set up an online community that quickly grew to have 50,000 members. They were very careful to not do anything about marketing because they realized that that the community was not about selling, but rather it was about conversing.

Waste of time you say? This company's community members were able to quickly identify what they were looking for but not finding in the company's products. They then went one step further (listen closely product managers) and **made product suggestions** that would meet their needs.

The company implemented these suggestions and got a great response. Their community members were so excited about the updated products that they were asking where and when they could buy them and **if they could have the first opportunity to buy them**. Man, don't we all wish that our customers were as excited about our products?

Chapter 9

When Times Are Bad – Product Managers Get Noticed!

Chapter 9: When Times Are Bad – Product Managers Get Noticed!

The economy dips even farther down each and every day if you are to believe what you read on the front page of just about every paper lately. Product Mangers are finding themselves in tighter and tighter situations – what can we do in these tough times **to make our products successful**. Would you believe that you already have the answer?

Martin Roth and Richard Ettenson over at the Wall Street Journal have been doing some digging in order to find out how product managers can **make the best of tumultuous times**. They've interviewed lots of folks including product managers who live in emerging markets and who have to deal with inflation, hyperinflation, or even recessions.

What they found is that these folks have remembered the golden rule of product management: it's **always easier to keep customers that you already have** instead of trying to get new customers. This means that when bad times arrive, these product mangers use their limited marketing dollars to draw their existing customers closer.

If you were planning on doing any broadcast marketing for your product on TV, on the radio, or even in magazines, then you might want to reconsider. This type of product advertising is generally geared towards informing potential customers. What you want to be doing is making your product(s) more visible and more available **to customers who already know about them**.

One key area that could have a great ROI (return-on-investment) for your product is **customer service**. You should always have good customer service, but when times get bad you should have great customer service. During tough times stop trying to up sell customers when they call customer service and instead start trying to help them make your product last longer. When things turn around, they'll remember you and you'll be glad that you helped them out.

Chapter 10

What Product Managers Can Learn From The Tropicana Mistake

Chapter 10: What Product Managers Can Learn From The Tropicana Mistake

In the world of product managers, there are some events that are only spoken about in hushed tones. Examples of product manager decisions that, when seen in the rear view mirror of time, just seem so very, very wrong that you wonder why the decision was ever made. Up until now the poster product for this kind of MAJOR screw-up has always been **new Coke**. However, someone has taken its place – Tropicana.

The Problem

The Tropicana company sells orange juice. They've got a big problem with their product: **you can't see the juice that you are buying**. It's pretty much the only prominent orange juice brand that is NOT sold in a transparent bottle.

The Solution

In order to solve this problem, Tropican reached to marketing and design guru Peter Arnell. Arnell has a long list of successful product designs to his credit including DKNY, Tommy Hilfiger and The Home Depot. He has an approach to branding that he calls PowerBranding that he has developed and uses with his customers. He's quite good at what he does.

For Topicana, Arnell added a **picture of a glass of orange juice** to the front of the carton. Now you could see the product. Sounds like a winner, eh?

The Fallout

Well, the new product packaging design went over like a lead balloon. The public was **outraged** – the Internet blew up with critics and not satisfied with just bashing the new design, folks also went after Arnell. What was up with this?

It turns out that Tropicana customers had some very deep associations with the way that the product looked. With the new design, something that had been so very familiar was all of a sudden **very strange**. There's no arguing that the new design was well thought out (new Coke was well thought out also), but the product manager had not asked customers the key question: is it ok if I change the design?

Lessons Learned

Not all products have this kind of bonding with their customers, but it's the **responsibility** of the product manager to check – you wouldn't want to become the next Tropicana-like disaster.

Chapter 11

How Product Managers Can Make Their Web Site Work For Their Product

Chapter 11: How Product Managers Can Make Their Web Site Work For Their Product

Who doesn't love the Internet? I mean **YOU** spend time there – doesn't the rest of the world do the same thing? Sure there are lots of things that you can do to promote your product just by using web-based social networking tools, but what about a website for your product?

If you can get over the daydream of you becoming and overnight billionaire by inventing the next Google / Facebook / Twitter and instead **focus on your product** for just a moment, the possibilities seem endless. But where to start?

The Wrong Way To Build A Product Web Site

I'm going to bet that your firm **already has a web site** that talks about your product in some shape or form. I'm also going to hazard a guess that you're not terribly happy with the way that it looks or works (or doesn't) today.

According to Marc Levitt from the MSLK graphic design firm, the **WRONG** way to go about correcting this problem is to just charge on in and decide that by adding Flash / Air / XML to your site everything will be better.

In fact, Marc says that the #1 mistake that most firms make is to start a product's web site design / redesign **without having a clear plan** of what they want to accomplish.

It's All About The Plan, Man

You better than anyone else should know that **you should never start ANY project without having at least some sort of plan**. When it comes to promoting your product on a web site there are all sorts of key issues that you need to answer in your plan such as how to easily navigate the site, what kind of content you want to include, and how you want to go about marketing your product.

When planning out how your web site is going to look / work, you'll want to create what is called a "wireframe". This is basically a text version of your web site, sorta like a **blueprint** of a building, that lays out how your product's web site will work BEFORE you invest in building the real deal. Needless to say, this is the correct time to make changes to the design – it will be **much more expensive** to change things later on.

Forget The Technology, Focus On The Message

Have you ever seen one of those Pixar movies? What's interesting is that they are not the only company making great looking animated movies. However, they are the best at doing it. The reason for this is because even though they use fantastic technology to create their movies they have never forgotten the key to a great movie – **it's all about the story**.

When it comes to your product's web site, it's all about the story – not the technology. Just because your competition has created a spectacular "splash page" that has everyone talking about how cool it is, don't allow yourself to become distracted. Marc reminds us that a site that is easy to **navigate** and that has been **designed well** always wins over a site with the latest in cool technology.

Next Steps

Marc has more suggestions for us; however, you've got plenty to work with for now. The #1 place to start is to create a **good plan** that will deliver to you a web site that actually works for your product. It may be very hard to resist wanting to load your new web site with every **new technology** out there just to give it a great "look", but resist you must. Ease of navigation and good content will **win the race** every time.

Chapter 12

Product Promotion Using The Web: Tricks For Product Managers

Chapter 12: Product Promotion Using The Web: Tricks For Product Managers

The promise of the Internet in its early days was that it was "**always on**". This meant that as you worked on other things (and slept), your product's web site was always out there selling, selling, selling your product to whomever happened to be looking at it. Sounds great, doesn't it?

Why Isn't Your Web Site Working For Your Product?

Over time we've all discovered the harsh reality of life that not all web sites are created equal – **some work, and some don't**. For some odd reason, we always seen to be checking out the web site of products that compete against our product and our heart is filled with envy.

According to Marc Levitt from the MSLK graphic design firm, there are a number of **WRONG** way to go about correcting this problem and just a few **RIGHT** ways to do it. Let's see if we can get some guidance on what to do after you've created a plan for updating your product's web site.

Don't Go It Alone – Get Buy-In

Just like when you are developing a new product, it's critical that you get inputs from everyone who will be affected by your redesigned product web site. The reason for doing this is because if you don't, then there is a very good chance that a major stakeholder **will show up at the last minute** and either kill your plans or end up changing everything that you've agreed to.

Get Customer Input

Is this starting to sound more and more like new product development? You wouldn't go out and create a new product without talking with your customers, so why would you change your product's web site without talking with them? Specifically, you want to find out what is and is not working with the current design. Your customers are the **only ones** who can tell you this.

Provide A Freshness Guarantee

What's the ultimate goal of your product's web site? Hopefully it's to increase sales. However, you can't expect your customers to buy the first time that they visit your product's site. Instead, you're going to have to assume that they'll have to visit it several times while they make up their minds. This means that you need to keep the content of your web site **up-to-date** and make sure that there is **fresh material** there on a regular basis. Remember: content is king

Final Thoughts

Your product's web site can do what you once dreamed that it would do for you: **promote your product 24×7**. However, an out-of-date web site that was designed years ago and which hasn't been updated since then won't be able to do this. Carefully planning an upgrade by working with ALL stakeholders and customers to create a new design that you keep fresh with updated content is your ticket to product success.

It's from the forge of failure that the steel of success is formed.

Hard Work Does Not Guarantee Success, But Success Does Not Happen Without Hard Work.

- Dr. Jim Anderson

Create Products Your Customers Want At A Price That They Are Willing To Pay!

Dr. Jim Anderson is available to provide training and coaching on the two topics that are the most important to product managers everywhere: how do I create the products that my customers want and what should I price them at?

Dr. Anderson believes that in order to both learn and remember what he says, product managers need to laugh. Each one of his speeches is full of fun and humor so that what he says "sticks" with everyone.

Dr. Anderson's Product Management Training Includes:

1. How can you segment your market?
2. What problems are your customers having right now?
3. Which of your customer's problems does your product solve?
4. How much of this problem does your product solve?
5. How much will it cost your customer if they don't fix this problem?

Dr. Jim Anderson presents over 100 speeches per year. To invite Dr. Anderson to speak at your event, contact him at:

Phone: 813-418-6970 or
Email: jim@BlueElephantConsulting.com

Blue Elephant Consulting

Speaking. Negotiating. Managing. Marketing.

Photo Credits:

Chapter 8 – By: Stew Dean
https://www.flickr.com/photos/stewdean/

Chapter 9 – By: Light Brigading
https://www.flickr.com/photos/40969298@N05/

Chapter 10 – By: j_lai
https://www.flickr.com/photos/jlai321/

Chapter 11 – By: Nate Weigle
https://www.flickr.com/photos/weiglen/

Chapter 12 – By: Pic Basement
https://www.flickr.com/photos/128199777@N08/

Other Books By The Author

Product Management

- Product Management Secrets: Techniques For Product Managers To Boost Product Sales And Increase Customer Satisfaction

- Product Development Lessons For Product Managers: How Product Managers Can Create Successful Products

- Customer Lessons For Product Managers: Techniques For Product Managers To Better Understand What Their Customers Really Want

- Product Failure Lessons For Product Managers: Examples Of Products That Have Failed For Product Managers To Learn From

- Communication Skills For Product Managers: The Communication Skills That Product Managers Need To Know How To Use In Order To Have A Successful Product

- How To Have A Successful Product Manager Career: The Things That You Need To Be Doing TODAY In Order To Have A Successful Product Manager Career

- Product Manager Product Success: How to keep your product on track and make it become a success

Public Speaking

- How To Become A Better Speaker By Changing How You Speak: Change techniques that will transform a speech into a memorable event

- How To Give A Great Presentation: Presentation techniques that will transform a speech into a memorable event

- How To Rehearse In Order To Give The Perfect Speech: How to effectively rehearse your next speech to that your message be remembered forever!

- Secrets To Creating The Perfect Speech: How to create a speech that will make your message be remembered forever!

- Secrets To Organizing The Perfect Speech: How to organize the best speech of your life!

- Secrets To Planning The Perfect Speech: How to plan to give the best speech of your life

- How To Show What You Mean During A Presentation: How to use visual techniques to transform a speech into a memorable event

CIO Skills

- What CIOs Need To Know About Working With Partners: Techniques For CIOs To Use In Order To Be Able To Successfully Work With Partners

- Critical CIO Management Skills: Decision Making Skills That Every CIO Needs To Have In Order To Be Able To Make The Right Choices

- How CIOs Can Make Innovation Happen: Tips And Techniques For CIOs To Use In Order To Make Innovation Happen In Their IT Department

- CIO Communication Skills Secrets: Tips And Techniques For CIOs To Use In Order To Become Better Communicators

- Managing Your CIO Career: Steps That CIOs Have To Take In Order To Have A Long And Successful Career

- CIO Business Skills: How CIOs can work effectively with the rest of the company!

IT Manager Skills

- How IT Managers Can Make Innovation Happen: Tips And Techniques For IT Managers To Use In Order To Make Innovation Happen In Their Teams

- Staffing Skills IT Managers Must Have: Tips And Techniques That IT Managers Can Use In Order To Correctly Staff Their Teams

- Secrets Of Effective Leadership For IT Managers: Tips And Techniques That IT Managers Can Use In Order To Develop Leadership Skills

- IT Manager Career Secrets: Tips And Techniques That IT Managers Can Use In Order To Have A Successful Career

- IT Manager Budgeting Skills: How IT Managers Can Request, Manage, Use, And Track Their Funding

Negotiating

- Learn How To Signal In Your Next Negotiation: How To Develop The Skill Of Effective Signaling In A Negotiation In Order To Get The Best Possible Outcome

- Learn The Skill Of Exploring In A Negotiation: How To Develop The Skill Of Exploring What Is Possible In A Negotiation In Order To Reach The Best Possible Deal

- Learn How To Argue In Your Next Negotiation: How To Develop The Skill Of Effective Arguing In A Negotiation In Order To Get The Best Possible Outcome

- How To Open Your Next Negotiation: How To Start A Negotiation In Order To Get The Best Possible Outcome

- Preparing For Your Next Negotiation: What You Need To Do BEFORE A Negotiation Starts In Order To Get The Best Possible Deal

- Learn How To Package Trades In Your Next Negotiation

Miscellaneous

- The Internet-Enabled Successful School District Superintendent: How To Use The Internet To Boost Parental Involvement In Your Schools

- Power Distribution Unit (PDU) Secrets: What Everyone Who Works In A Data Center Needs To Know!

- Making The Jump: How To Land Your Dream Job When You Get Out Of College!

- How To Use The Internet To Create Successful Students And Involved Parents

"Practical, proven examples of how to use your marketing skills to make your product a success!"

This book has been written with one goal in mind – to show you how to use your marketing skills to make your product fly off the shelves. We're going to show you how to make sure that this job turns into a success for you!

Let's Make Your Career A Success!

<u>**What You'll Find Inside:**</u>

- **PRODUCT MANAGER MARKETING MISTAKES**

- **HOW TO USE WEB 2.0 TO BE A BETTER PRODUCT MANAGER**

- **HOW PRODUCT MANAGERS CAN GET BETTER AT CREATING POWERPOINT SLIDES**

- **PRODUCT MANAGERS & THE SECRET OF THE COLOR WHEEL**

Dr. Jim Anderson brings his 4 college degrees coupled with over 25 years of real-world experience to this book. He's managed products at some of the world's largest firms as well as at start-ups. He's going to show you what you need to do in order to make your career a success!

www.ingramcontent.com/pod-product-compliance
Lightning Source LLC
Chambersburg PA
CBHW070945180526
45168CB00003B/1169